I belong to Leafs Nation™!

_____

The HOME Team

Toronto Maple Leafs®

Written by Holly Preston
Illustrated by Val Lawton

Always Books Ltd.

The Home Team: Toronto Maple Leafs®

Text © 2014 Holly Preston
Illustrations © 2014 Val Lawton

Manufactured by Friesens Corporation in Altona, MB, Canada
May 2014
Job # 201908

Preston, Holly, author
The home team : Toronto Maple Leafs / written by Holly Preston ; illustrated by Val Lawton.

(The home team Toronto Maple Leafs)
ISBN 978-0-9869244-4-6 (bound)

1. Toronto Maple Leafs (Hockey team)--Juvenile literature.
I. Lawton, Val, 1962-, illustrator II. Title.

PS8631.R467H643 2014   jC813'.6   C2014-902105-4

Layout by Heather Nickel, Your Nickel's Worth Publishing

Always Books Ltd.

AFANFORLIFE.COM

For all young LEAFS™ fans
who know there's no team like ours!

There was nothing better than playing hockey …

… except watching hockey when the **TORONTO MAPLE LEAFS**® played.

Ethan played defence. Liam played forward. Noah was in goal.
The boys played different positions. They had the same dream:
to one day play for the **TORONTO MAPLE LEAFS**.

"Aren't they great?" said Liam, knowing his teammates would agree.

"The **LEAFS**™ are great passers," said Ethan. "And great scorers," added Noah.

He wondered what it would be like to be in goal against them!

How could I ever play for the **TORONTO MAPLE LEAFS**®*?* Liam wondered.
His sister Olivia was already the best goal scorer in the neighbourhood.

And Liam never scored. Ever.
The puck went high. The puck went low.
The puck went everywhere but where it was supposed to go.

"You know, Liam," his dad said, "the **LEAFS**™ were little boys once, too. They didn't become hockey stars overnight. You can learn a lot by watching what the **LEAFS**™ do."

The **LEAFS**™ skate *fast.*

They make big plays.

They shoot. They score!

And make a million saves.

Liam knew the only way to get better was to practise.
Becoming one of the **TORONTO MAPLE LEAFS**® wouldn't be easy,
but he believed it *could* happen.

"Kids," said Liam and Olivia's dad, "who wants to go to a **LEAFS**™ practice?"
Of course, they all did.

Liam, Ethan, Noah and Olivia were excited to be so close
to the **TORONTO MAPLE LEAFS**®. They stayed until all the players were off the ice.

On the way back to the car, Ethan saw something.

"This belongs to my favourite player. I'd recognize his good luck charm anywhere," Ethan said. "Let's take it to the stadium and turn it in right away."

"You did the right thing. You deserve tickets to tonight's **LEAFS**™ game,"
said the lady at the Air Canada Centre.
"That's the luckiest charm ever!" said Olivia.

They couldn't have imagined what would happen next!

It was an action-packed game.

Liam seized the moment.

"What does it take to play for the **TORONTO MAPLE LEAFS**®?" he asked.

Believe.

Play like a team…

...and with heart.

Celebrate when your teammate plays well.

And never give up.

Noah said, "I'm going to be a **LEAFS**™ fan forever."
The others knew they would be, too.

The next morning they got up early to play. Liam didn't get a goal. He got *five* goals!
Ethan, Noah and especially Olivia were happy. But they weren't surprised.
The team had believed in him all along.

Liam felt really good about playing hockey. And he had another good feeling, too.
"This is the year our **TORONTO MAPLE LEAFS**® will win the Stanley Cup®!"

ABOUT THE AUTHOR
Holly Preston

Holly Preston is a journalist who worked for CTV and CBC. She grew up watching NHL hockey with her brother and father. Now she creates children's picture books for professional sports teams. She hopes Leafs™ fans will enjoy having a book that celebrates their home team and encourages young fans to find a love of reading.

ABOUT THE ILLUSTRATOR
Val Lawton

Val Lawton is an artist, an artist-educator with the Learning Through the Arts Program, and a children's book illustrator. The Home Team: Toronto Maple Leafs™ is her 25th book. This is the fifth time she and author Holly Preston have teamed up to celebrate Canadian sports.

We dedicate this book to our brothers,
Leafs™ fans forever.

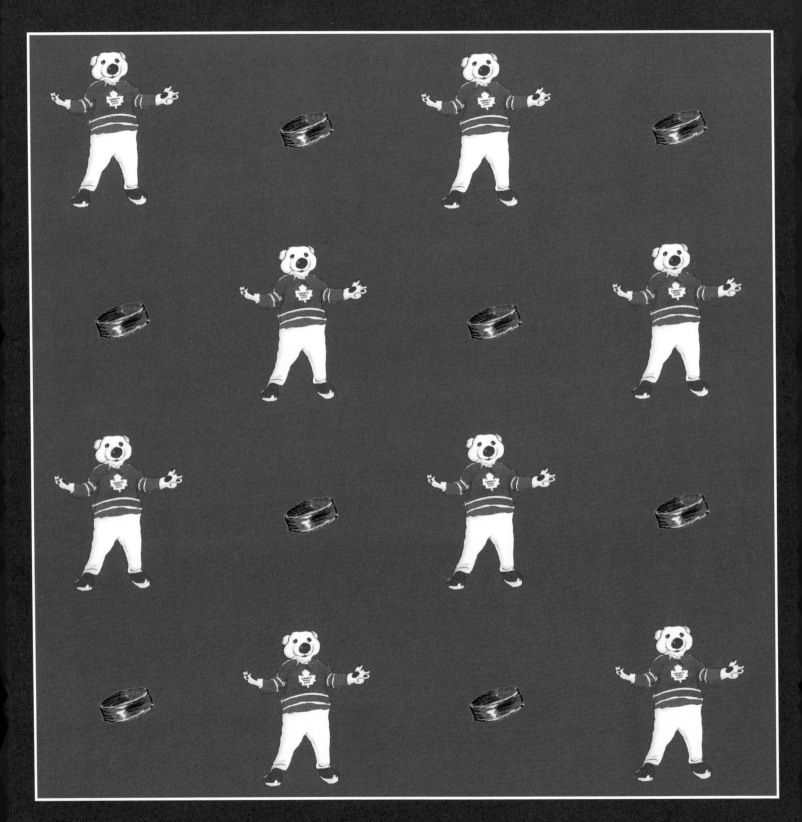